TOTALLY

TACKY

CARTOONS

by Rick Detorie

A Wallaby Book
Published by Simon & Schuster, Inc.
Distributed by Simon & Schuster

Special thanks to Susan and Dwaine
Tinsley and John Billette for their help
and support and winsome warped wisdom.

First Wallaby Books printing November 1983

10 9 8 7 6 5 4 3 2 1

Manufactured in the United States of America

ISBN: 0-671-50083-X

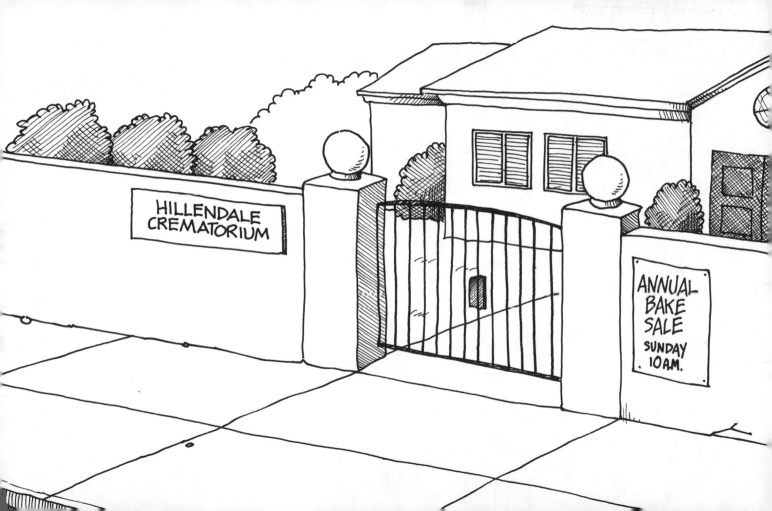

Ladies' League Nite
ROSIE'S ROLLERS
ROSIE'S ROLLERS
ROSIE'S ROLLERS
ALICE'S ANOREXICS
ALICE'S ANOREXICS